Kaimana the Hawaiian Mermaid

TARA COYOTE & NICA QUINN

Edited by Skye Blue Press: Skyebluepress.com

Formatted by Jen Henderson of WildWordsFormatting.com

This is the coloring book version of the original Kaiamana the Hawaiian Mermaid book. You can find the colored version of the same book on Amazon.

For the future generations of children
and all of the world's ocean inhabitants.

My wish is that you witness the wild beauty of the ocean,
swim in her splendor and enjoy her marine life,
as I have been fortunate to experience in my lifetime.

May all of Earth's creatures thrive
as they rightfully deserve to!

Foreword

In a world where humans are learning to be Earth's greatest allies, join our young hero on a journey to protect our precious planet. Amidst the challenges of today's world, they discover the power of positivity and action. With the help of beautiful illustrations that paint a picture of a harmonious and colorful ocean, this tale reminds us to imagine the best possible future, channel our energy into action, and make choices that dance in harmony with our planet. Dive into this inspiring adventure and learn how you too can be a guardian of our vibrant, living Earth.

~ Hannah Mermaid

Once upon a time

there was a small, round island, in the middle of the Pacific Ocean. This island was a utopia of unprecedented delight with frolicking fish, colorful flowers, and delicious tropical fruits. All was idyllic and perfect on this island paradise.

Kaimana lived with her beloved merfolk friends, the fish, turtles, whales, dolphins, and a myriad of life under the sea— they were free.

For many generations, Kaimana's merfolk ancestors lived in harmony with the human and animal creatures of the lands and the oceans.

They lived simply and sustainably, receiving the abundance that nature had given them, while giving back in return. They were always grateful for the many gifts they were given.

In Kaimana's generation, the pristine ocean environment slowly began to change, alarming the merfolk. The colorful coral reefs where the fish called home began to fade. Algae grew on the corals, and their beautiful colors soon changed to a bleached out white.

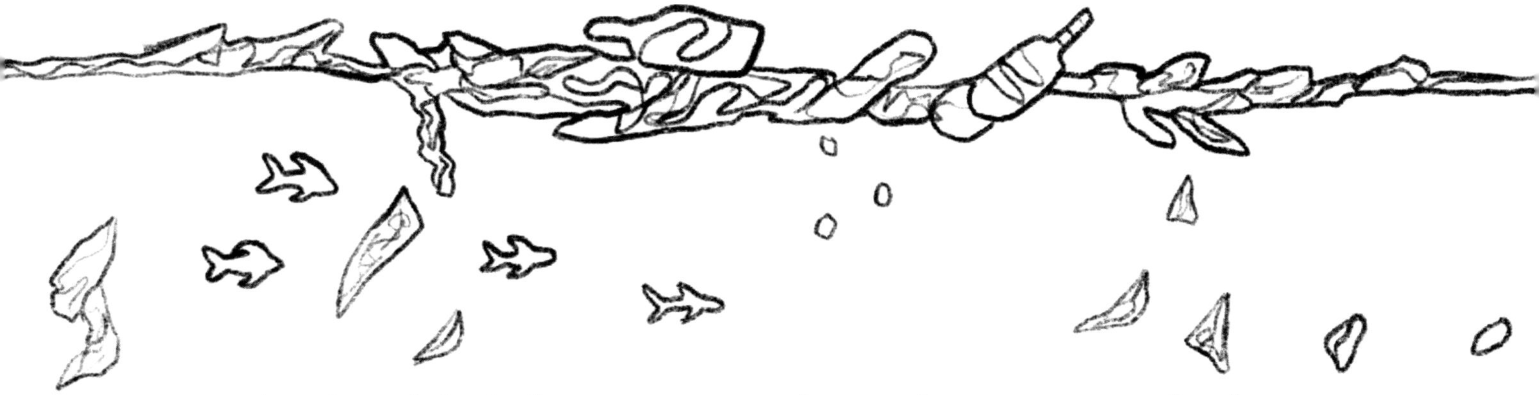

Floating debris from man-made products encroached on their underwater homes, and trash floated thousands of miles from many faraway lands. All the creatures of the ocean were affected—in subtle and significant ways. Sadly, some would mistake plastic for food.

Whales inhabit the vast body of the ocean's domain.
The whales that visit the Hawaiian Islands are:

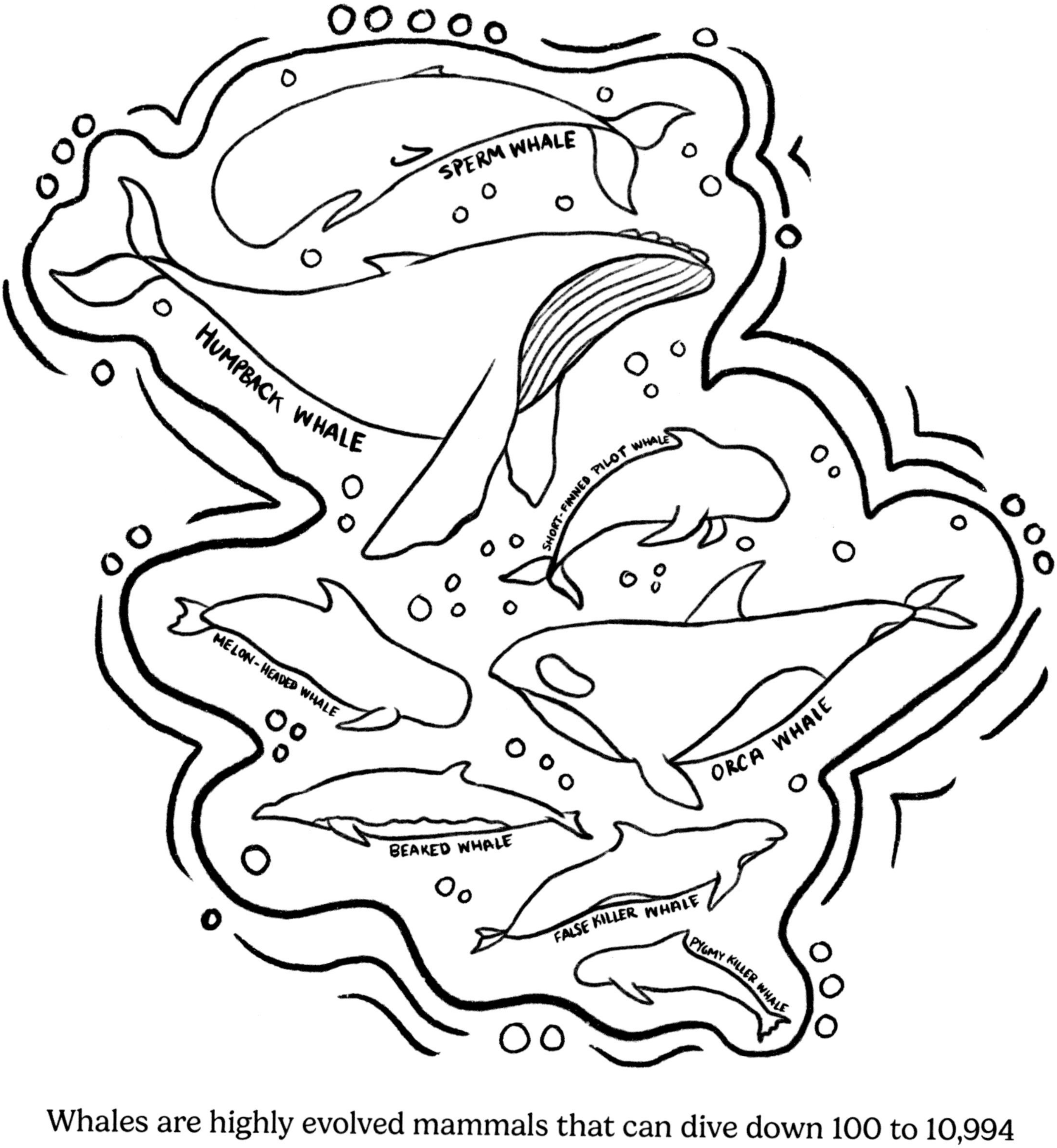

Whales are highly evolved mammals that can dive down 100 to 10,994 meters—328 to 32,808 feet deep, depending on the whale. Whale songs are incredibly complex and sound waves of their songs can travel thousands of miles through the body of the ocean.

One day, a rare and magnificent sperm whale washed up on the shore of Kaimana's oceanic home. Humans, merfolk and all the ocean creatures grieved the loss of its life. The beautiful creature, a gentle giant, had choked on fishing nets and various plastic items.

The death of the whale greatly impacted Kaimana and her ocean friends. For thousands of years, the mermaids and mermen had lived in harmony with the whales. To lose one of their wise friends from the foibles of human consumption was a harsh wake up call. They had to do something!

Kaimana also realized her fish friends were eating the bits of floating plastic because they thought it was food. She knew this would also make her human friends sick when they ate the polluted fish. Kaimana knew how harmful these colorful pieces of man-made materials were. She felt powerless.

Kaimana and her friends decided to do something about this tragedy! She could not stand by and watch her magical ocean world be ruined. Kaimana gathered the young and old merfolk together to share ideas about creating a solution for plastic pollution.

As the mermaids and mermen gathered, the ocean creatures came together, curious to see what they were talking about. The fish, turtles, dolphins, and even some whales, listened in and shared their opinions!

The merfolk worked together with the humans to bring awareness to stopping plastic pollution. Through a massive island campaign, they inspired the human beings to reduce their plastic intake and use sustainable methods instead of relying on plastic.

They encouraged people to:

A. Instead of buying single use plastics, they taught others to use metal and glass containers for carrying food.

B. To stop buying plastic when possible, or if it was purchased to re-use it as long as possible.

C. Once it is no longer useful, make sure it is recycled.

Through Kaimana's, the merfolk and the human's efforts, they once again restored harmony to the natural environment of their fragile island ecosystem. This not only created a safe haven for all the ocean creatures but helped create balance for the humans and the land creatures.

Around the world, the word spread of the efforts of the island community with reducing plastic intake and helping to create a safe environment for all the ocean creatures. Other countries became inspired to reduce their plastic intake, which helped to create balance for whales and ocean creatures around the entire globe.

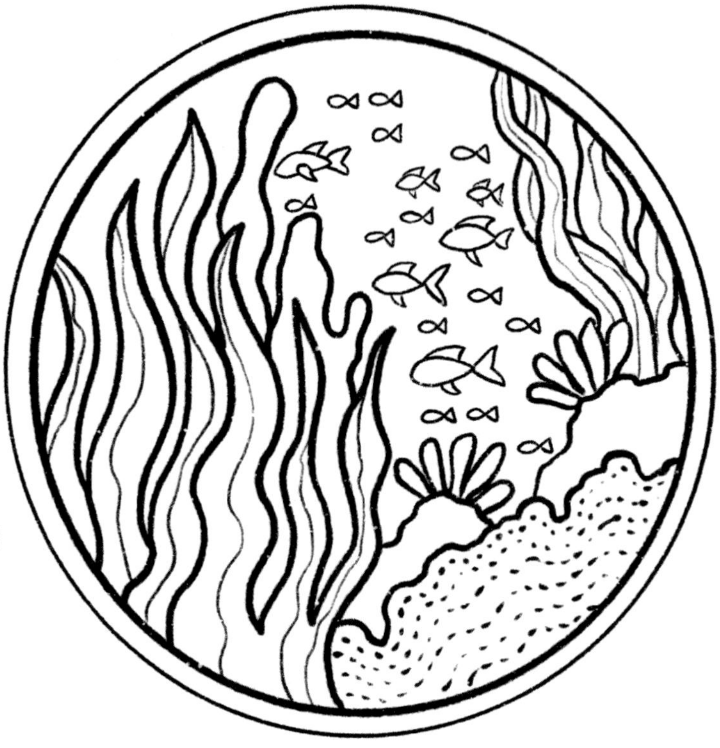

We are now at a tipping point and every individual upon
this precious planet has a chance to make a difference.
Do you want this reality or this one?

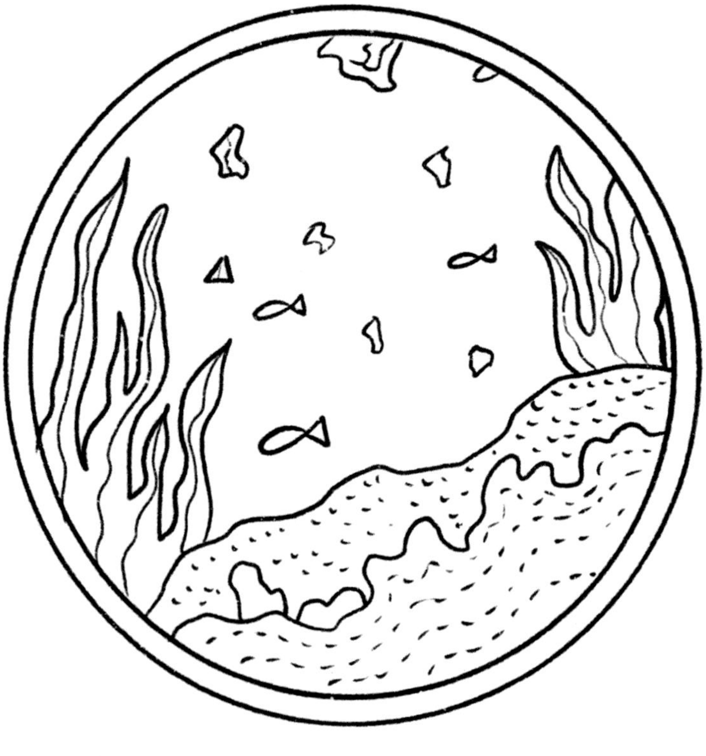

The Earth is in your hands. WE ALL can make a change for a healthy future for all creatures: humans, animals, ocean creatures, merfolk and the Earth. What can you do to make a difference?

Note from the Author

I choose the name Kaimana for the main character as in Hawaiian it is an auspicious name which can be broken down as "kai" which means "ocean" and "mana" translates to "power" or "spiritual energy of the ocean". This linguistic connection highlights the deep ties between the name and the natural world, reflecting the importance of the ocean in Hawaiian culture. Kaimana, with its deep ties to the ocean and the forces of nature, held a special place in the hearts of the Hawaiian people.

During ancient times (pre-colonization era), Kaimana was not just a name but a symbol of strength and resilience. It represented the courage and determination of the Hawaiian people in the face of adversity. The name Kaimana was often given to children who were believed to possess exceptional qualities and destined for greatness. It was a name that carried the weight of history and the hopes of future generations.

As the ancient Hawaiians navigated the vast Pacific Ocean, they looked to Kaimana as a guiding light, a beacon of hope in times of uncertainty. In our turbulent time on Earth, this seemed like an appropriate name for such a courageous character.

I have great respect for the Native Hawaiian culture. As my father's Portuguese side of our family dates back to the 1870's on Kaua'i, Hawaii and I have lived many years on The Garden Island, I have been well aware of the tragic decimation of the Hawaiian race and loss of culture by colonization. My attempt to have Nica, the artist, represent Hawaiians as the dominant mermaid and merman race in this book is a show of respect for the wisdom they hold for the 'aina – earth.

Why I Wrote This Book

At a young age, I knew my parents were different than my other friends' parents. I thought they were weird and called them "nature nuts." As I grew older, I understood how fortunate my brother and I were to be raised by ardent environmentalists that cared passionately for the Earth and her creatures. Now I know they were way before their time and lo and behold, I grew up to be a "nature nut" too!

My mother, Gail Cheeseman, was a recycling pioneer and a lot like Kaimana, in this book. Long before it was cool to recycle, my mother single handedly in the late 1970's started a recycling drive at my elementary school by renting a large container and mobilizing the entire community to bring in their recycled goods. This was unheard of during this time!

My father, Doug Cheeseman, was a biology professor at De Anza College in the Bay Area, California, for 30 years. Both my parents promoted how important it was to value and care about the earth, before being an environmentalist was hip! My father would give environmental talks all around the Santa Clara Valley area, talking about our precious earth and her creatures. They created Cheesemans' Ecology Safaris, a safari company that continues to lead environmentally based safaris around the globe to educate about the rich biodiversity and diverse birds and mammals upon the Earth.

This photo was taken in around 2002 after a family whale watching trip in Monterey Bay, CA that my parents and brother led. I treasure these memories. Note: My brother Ted is gently choking my son, Willow in a big bear hug!

I share the story about my parents, as their love of the earth influenced me in a positive manner. They both tragically died in November 2021 (mother) and March 2022 (father), which heavily impacted me. My world was utterly rocked after their deaths. In many ways, this book is a tribute to them for the environmental zeal they infused within me.

My beloved father was from Kapa'a, Kaua'i, Hawai'i, where I am fortunate to live now. After his death, rediscovering my love of being in the water was the most effective healing for my grief-stricken heart. Not only did I start to swim frequently in the luminous tropical water of the Garden Island, but I discovered the joy of wearing a mermaid tail!

From a young age, I have been fascinated with mermaid art, stories, legend and lore. Being in the water has been my safe place and how I processed my emotions. To embrace the art of being a mermaid, when my heart was shattered after my parents passing, was my way of reclaiming myself again.

As I swam in the idyllic water of the Hawaiian Islands, with the turtles and colorful fish, I realized that most people do not understand the importance of a healthy, marine ecosystem. The ocean is a mysterious, magnificent force in her colossal wonder. People all around the globe marvel at the ocean's beauty, but in general do not understand the rich life that dwells miles under its surface. There are creatures living at great depths that have not even been discovered yet, as humans have not been able to reach them.

The part in this book about the sperm whale washing up on the coast of Kaua'i, Hawai'i is absolutely true! On January 27, 2023, a 56-foot (17-meter) long, 120,000-pound (54,400-kilogram) sperm whale washed up at Lydgate Park on the east side of the island in Wailua. Its stomach contained: six hagfish traps, seven types of fishing nets, two types of plastic bags, a light protector, fishing line and a float from a net. It was sadly choked by these man-made materials that created a blockage in the whale's intestinal track, which blocked the whale from absorbing food. Sperm whales are a rare and enigmatic species due to their ability to dive deeper than the usual humpback whales that are usually seen around the Hawaiian Islands during the winter mating season. (*Read the whale section for more information about this!)* Like Kaimana, in the book, the sperm whale's death was gravely disturbing to me.

After the success of Nica Quinn (Ware) and my first children's picture book, *Comanche the Wild Mustang*, (published in 2022) I knew I had to do something with my author platform to speak up about the importance of preserving our fragile ocean ecosystem and the whale calamity that unfolded here on Kaua'i.

The ocean and her creatures deserve to a healthy ocean to live in. In fact, our future as a human species depends on a vibrant ocean environment. We are not separate from the ocean. Down to the smallest bacterial creature to the largest blue whale in the ocean, our human habits impact their delicate existence. Even though we may not see the endless forms of life that dwell miles beneath the ocean floor, our everyday actions play a part in their survival.

The "7th generation" principle taught by Native Americans says that in every decision, be it personal, governmental or corporate, we must consider how it will affect our descendants seven generations into the future. The purpose of this is to ensure that our abundant earth will still be here for future generations to enjoy. It is vital to shift our thinking as a society to this perspective for the health of our grandchildren, the earth, and all of her creatures!

My greatest hope is that this book will add to this shift in global awareness, and aid others in making the choices that will help preserve the beauty we experience today, for the people and creatures of tomorrow to enjoy.

Conservation Information

Whale Information:

As this book is whale-centered, it is important to share some fascinating information about these mysterious creatures. While there are 94 species of whales on our diverse planet, I have chosen to focus on sperm and humpback whales, as they are the main cetaceans in this book and humpback whales have the most prominent presence here on the Hawaiian Islands.

Sperm Whales:

Sperm whales are the largest of the toothed whales and have one of the widest global distributions of any marine mammal species. They are found in all deep oceans, from the equator to the edge of the pack ice in the Arctic and Antarctic.

Sperm whales have the largest brain in the world, which is over six times larger than the human brain! This means sperm whales develop social connections, culture and bonding associated with mammals with larger and more complex brains.

Historical evidence suggests that sperm whales share information about how to avoid whalers and alter their behavior to survive. For example, sperm whales were able to realize that their usual method of circling an attacker wouldn't work against the new threat of whaling ships. Instead, they would swim upwind, realizing their hunters needed a favoring wind to chase after them. The result of these clever new whale strategies was a 58%

drop in a whaler's success in harpooning a whale, learning that was shared between whale family groups!

These exceptional animals can hold their breath and stay submerged for well over an hour, diving down to depths of 4,000 feet (1,219 meters) in search of prey. That's about the height of three Empire State Buildings stacked down below the waves!

Sperm whales are named after the waxy substance—spermaceti—found in their heads. The spermaceti is an oil sac that helps the whales focus sound, and was used in oil lamps, candles, and lubricants. This made them a primary target of the commercial whaling industry from 1800 to 1987, which nearly eliminated all the world's large whale populations. While whaling is no longer a major threat, sperm whale populations are still recovering. The sperm whale is listed as endangered under the Endangered Species Act and depleted under the Marine Mammal Protection Act, two critical laws that have helped many species return from near-extinction.

Humpback Whales:

Humpback whales live in all the oceans of the world. They travel great distances every year and have one of the longest migrations of any mammal on the planet. *(Read more about migration below.)* Humpback whales feed on shrimp-like crustaceans (krill) and small fish, straining huge volumes of ocean water through their baleen plates, which act like a sieve.

It is common to see them in the Hawaiian Islands from December to April. This period coincides with the humpback whales' annual migration from their feeding grounds in the cold, nutrient-rich waters of Alaska, Russia and Canada to the warm, shallow waters surrounding Hawai'i.

The main reason humpback whales migrate to Hawai'i is for breeding and calving. The warm waters of Hawai'i provide a gathering place for their social mating behavior, and a safe and comfortable environment for

female humpbacks to give birth to their calves. The shallow, protected bays and coastal areas offer protection from predators, reducing the risk of calf predation.

During the winter months, male humpback whales actively engage in courtship rituals to attract females. These courtship behaviors can include breaching (leaping out of the water), tail slapping, large group 'competitive chases', and singing their mesmerizing songs. This makes the winter season an excellent time to witness the awe-inspiring displays of acrobatics and hear the hauntingly beautiful songs of the humpback whales.

Before a final moratorium on commercial whaling in 1985, all populations of humpback whales were greatly reduced, most by more than 95 percent. The species has recovered throughout much of its global range, but faces threats from entanglement in fishing gear, vessel strikes, vessel-based harassment, underwater noise, and ocean warming from climate change.

Humpback whales can dive to depths of around 660 feet (200 meters) and can hold their breath for up to 30 minutes, but usually their breath hold is an average of 15 minutes.

The humpback whale gets its common name from the distinctive hump on its back. Its long pectoral fins inspired its scientific name, *Megaptera*, which means "big-winged" and *novaeangliae*, which means "New England," in reference to the location where European whalers first encountered them. Humpback whales are a favorite of whale watchers—they are often active, jumping out of the water and slapping the surface with their pectoral fins or tails.

Whale Songs:

Whales are very social creatures that travel in groups called "pods." They use a variety of noises to communicate and socialize with each other. The three main types of sounds made by whales are clicks, whistles, and pulsed calls.

Clicks are made by toothed whales, sperm whales and their relatives, believed to be for navigation and identifying physical surroundings. When the sound waves bounce off of an object, they return to the whale, allowing the whale to identify the shape of the object. Clicks can even help to differentiate between friendly creatures and predators. Clicks are used frequently during social interactions, showing they are important for communication.

Whistles and pulsed calls are used during social activities. Pulsed calls are more frequent and sound like squeaks, screams, and squawks to the human ear. Differing vocal "dialects" have been found to exist between different pods within the same whale population. Some dolphin species have even been shown to have "signature whistles", which may be like names used to refer to each other as individuals.

Whales also use their tails and fins to make loud slapping noises on the surface of the water to communicate nonverbally. The sound can be heard for hundreds of meters below the surface and may be a warning sign of aggression or a tool to scare schools of fish together, making them an easier meal.

Humpback whales, and some other species of baleen whales, sing songs as complex as operas, singing continuously for many hours while in Hawai'i and other breeding areas. Nobody knows the meaning of these songs, but they must be an important part of their breeding behavior. Scientists have learned that all whales in an area sing the same song, with changes each season that all whales learn as part of a complex culture.

Migration:

When it comes to understanding the migration patterns of whales and figuring out why different species migrate in different ways, it is important to understand what the purpose for their migration is, because not all whales migrate for the same reasons.

Some whales will migrate in order to get to their local feeding or mating grounds, as they tend to have specific locations where they gather for these two different activities.

Most species of large whales migrate between feeding and mating seasons, to food-rich cooler waters during the warmer summer months and to warmer waters during the colder winter months in order to mate and give birth to their offspring. Many species of whales fast for months during their breeding seasons. Cold water supports more food – and large whales need enormous amounts of food – stored as blubber to be turned into energy and into milk to support nursing their calves. A humpback whale calf will grow 100 pounds (40 kilograms) and one inch (two centimeters) per day!

Some species of whales and dolphins do not migrate or make only short migrations. The ocean still holds many mysteries to be discovered by future scientists and explorers, and among these mysteries are the migrations – and reasons for migrating – for many species of whales that are poorly studied.

Sperm Whale Migration:

Female and young sperm whales live in family groups in tropical waters of all the world's oceans, resident or making small migrations to follow their main food, squid. Male sperm whales stay with family groups until approximately five to ten years old, then tend to migrate to colder waters toward polar regions. Here they find large squid and fish populations that helps them grow much larger than females; a large male sperm whale will grow to three times the size of his mother. Sperm whale migrations are not as predictable or well understood as migrations of humpback whales. Because male sperm whales leave their family groups for months or even years, but are very social and maintain strong family relationships, reunions when a male returns to tropical waters can be very exciting events.

Humpback Whale Migration:

Humpback whales can travel great distances during their seasonal migration with some animals migrating 5,000 miles (8,000 kilometers) between high-latitude summer feeding grounds and winter mating and calving areas in tropical waters. In the first months of a whale's life, they will migrate with their mother back to her favorite feeding areas, and will usually follow the same pattern as their mother for the rest of their life. In the North Pacific, some humpback whales migrate from Alaska to Hawai'i and can complete the 3,000-mile (5,000 kilometer) trip in as few as 28 days. While calving, they prefer shallow, warm waters commonly near offshore reef systems or shores. Humpback whale feeding grounds are generally in cold waters that support more of the krill and fish they love to feed on.

Threats to Whales:

Entanglement: Entanglement in fishing gear, ocean trash and other human-made objects underwater is a major danger to many marine animals, including whales. It is estimated that hundreds of thousands of whales die each year worldwide as a result of entanglements. Entanglement may result in starvation or drowning due to restricted movement, physical trauma, and systemic infections. An entangled animal also may not be able to feed, and may be more at risk to other threats, like vessel collisions.

Vessel Collisions: Whales are at risk of being hit by vessels. These collisions may result in serious injury and death to both humans and whales. Large ships carrying cargo or people travel at high speeds through the environments where whales must live and feed, a bit like if cars and trucks traveled right through your bedroom and living room.

Acoustic Disturbance: Marine animals rely on sound for communication, navigation, and feeding. Acoustic disturbances due to dredging, blasting, vessel traffic, active acoustics, and other activities affects whales like if bright lights were shining in your eyes wherever you look.

Marine Debris: Ocean trash is a growing issue worldwide for all sea creatures, like the example in this book with the sperm whale. Marine animals of all sizes suffer from ingesting plastic and other man-made materials.

Climate Change and Global Warming: Whales and dolphins depend on healthy oceans that support healthy fish, krill and squid populations. Warming waters support less food, which means less healthy oceans. As the global climate warms, oceans are absorbing heat and marine heatwaves are becoming more common, affecting food sources for whales.

Coral Reef Conservation

Coral Reefs are actually animals!

Because corals are attached, taking root to the seafloor, people often think they are plants. Because many corals have hardened surfaces, they are sometimes mistaken as being rocks. However, unlike plants, corals do not make their own food using photosynthesis (turning sunlight energy into food energy). And, unlike rocks, corals are very much alive. Corals are, in fact, animals. They are invertebrates (animals lacking a backbone) belonging to the phylum Cnidaria, class Anthozoa.

What we often call "a coral" is actually made up of hundreds or thousands of individual animals called polyps. The polyp uses calcium carbonate (limestone) from seawater to build a hard, cup-shaped skeleton. This skeleton protects the soft, delicate body of the polyp.

Each polyp has a stomach that opens at one end, which is surrounded by tentacles. The tentacles capture food by stinging it, similar to a jellyfish. Some corals also make homes for algae that give the corals their color and provides food through photosynthesis. This is called a "symbiotic" relationship. Coral reefs are complex and ancient habitats. They have been a feature of life on Earth for around 500 million years. They are a critical component of life in the ocean. Often referred to as "rainforests of the sea," coral reef ecosystems are one of the most biodiverse in the world.

Around 25% of all marine species rely on coral reefs, including sharks and sea turtles, crustaceans, and schooling fish. More than 7,000 species of fishes, invertebrates, plants, sea turtles, birds, and marine mammals can be found in the coral reef ecosystem.

Sadly, unless we humans make major changes to how we treat oceans, we stand to lose all shallow-water coral reefs by the end of this century.

Coral Reefs are Disappearing:

Although coral reefs have survived the last five mass extinctions, they can no longer keep up with the speed of global environmental changes caused by human activity.

We have lost more than half of the world's coral reefs in the last 30 years; without immediate action, all shallow water coral reefs are projected to vanish by the end of this century.

Reefs are under threat as a result of both local and global stressors. The combination of these threats is putting reefs under extreme pressure.

Impacts to life on Earth:

Losing all of our shallow water coral reefs would be like losing every rainforest on the planet. We don't yet know how catastrophic and complex the impacts of this would be, as humanity has never experienced the loss of an entire biome.

Around 70% of all atmospheric oxygen is produced by the ocean. Coral reefs are a critical part of the balance of life in the sea.

While there is no way to know how severe the consequences of losing all of our planet's coral reefs, we do know that losing coral reefs causes:

- Damage to coasts, shorelines, homes, and businesses
- Economic fallout from the loss of fishing and tourism
- The collapse of the balance of life in the oceans

Local stressors to coral reefs include direct physical damage, pollution, fishing, curio trade, disease, coastal development, plastics, invasive species and chemicals in sunscreen.

Climate change – global stressor:

Climate change is the single greatest threat to coral reefs stems from the increase of carbon dioxide in the air from human-made pollution.

Corals, like most animals, can only survive in a narrow temperature range. The ideal temperature range for coral is between 73- and 84-degrees Fahrenheit (22- and 29 Celsius) and Coral bleaching occurs when temperatures rise too far above this range.

The consistent rise in ocean temperature is making the frequency and severity of bleaching events worse, to the point where corals cannot recover.

Ocean acidification:

The absorption of atmospheric carbon dioxide also causes the ocean's pH to drop, becoming more acidic, creating a host of problems for marine life.

Acidification effectively "dissolves" a coral's calcium carbonate skeleton (think of tooth enamel in soda pop). The increase in carbon changes the water chemistry, causing an imbalance between the hydrogen and carbonate ions which makes producing a calcium carbonate skeleton significantly harder.

Plastic Damage to Coral Reefs:

The chances of disease on a coral reef are increased up to 22 times by plastics. In 2018, a huge survey of the 159 coral reefs across Asia-Pacific region showed that over 11.1 billion plastic particles are entangling the corals, and this number is estimated to increase dramatically by 40% by 2025. (*See more about this in the plastic section.*)

Curb the Plastic Addiction!

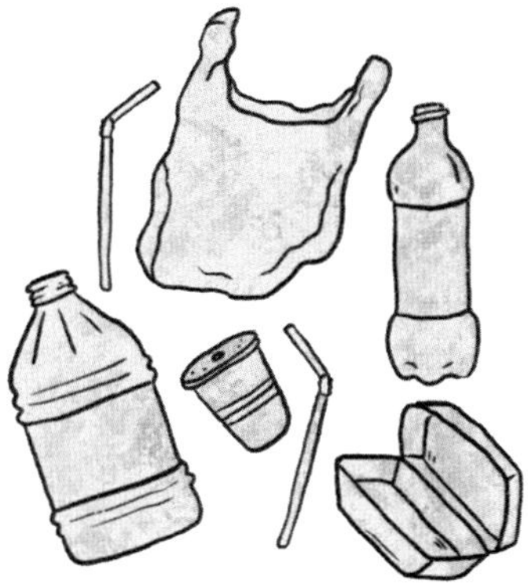

Plastic Reduction and Conservation

The billions upon billions of items of plastic waste choking our oceans, lakes, and rivers and piling up on land is more than unsightly and harmful to plants and wildlife.

The following facts shed light on how plastic is proving dangerous to our planet, health, and wildlife.

Microplastics in different forms are present in almost all water systems in the world, be they streams, rivers, lakes, or oceans. There is more microplastic in the ocean than there are stars in the Milky Way.

1. By 2050 there will be more plastic in the oceans than there are fish (by weight).

2. The chances of disease on a coral reef are enhanced by 22-fold by plastics. In 2018, a huge survey of the 159 coral reefs across Asia-Pacific region showed that over 11.1 billion plastic particles are entangling the corals, and this number is estimated to increase dramatically by 40% by 2025. Importantly, more than 7000 species of fishes, invertebrates, plants, sea turtles, birds, and marine mammals can be found in the coral reef

ecosystem. Ultimately plastic debris is choking our precious coral reef environment.

3. Animals are now colonizing the Great Pacific Garbage Patch, meaning that they are consuming the plastic waste and also living in previously uninhabited areas. All of these developments disrupt the natural marine ecosystem

4. Marine animals at the base of the food chain eat microplastics, which are then eaten by other marine life, which are then consumed by humans. This creates an unhealthy food chain, which ultimately is toxic to all that consume the seafood.

What are Microplastics and why are they dangerous?

Plastic is the most prevalent type of marine debris found in our oceans and large bodies of water around the earth. Plastic debris can come in all shapes and sizes, but those that are less than five millimeters in length (or about the size of a sesame seed) are called "microplastics."

Microplastics come from a variety of sources, including from larger plastic debris that degrades into smaller and smaller pieces. In addition, microbeads, a type of microplastic, are very tiny pieces of manufactured polyethylene plastic that are added as exfoliants to health and beauty products, such as some cleansers and toothpastes. These tiny particles easily pass through water filtration systems and end up in the oceans, posing a potential threat to aquatic life.

Microbeads are not a recent problem. According to the United Nations Environmental Programme, plastic microbeads first appeared in personal care products about fifty years ago, with plastics increasingly replacing natural ingredients. As recently as 2012, this issue was still relatively unknown, with an abundance of products containing plastic microbeads on the market and not a lot of awareness on the part of consumers.

In recent years, microplastics have been documented in all parts of the human lung, maternal and fetal placental tissues, human breast milk and in human blood.

The problem with microplastics is that—like plastic items of any size—they do not readily break down into harmless molecules. Plastics can take hundreds or thousands of years to decompose—and in the meantime, wreak havoc on the environment. On beaches, microplastics are visible as tiny multicolored plastic bits in sand. In the oceans, microplastic pollution is often consumed by marine animals.

Some of this environmental pollution is from littering, but much is the result of storms, water runoff, and winds that carry plastic—both intact objects and microplastics—into our oceans. Single-use plastics—plastic items meant to be used just once and then discarded, such as a straw—are the primary source of secondary plastics in the environment.

Though durable, plastics do degrade, by weathering from water, wind, sunlight or heat — as in ocean environments or in landfills — or by friction, in the case of car tires, which releases plastic particles along roadways during motion and braking.

What do we know about the potential health risks?

Studies in mice suggest microplastics are not benign. Research in these test animals shows that lab exposure to microplastics can disrupt the gut microbiome, lead to inflammation, lower sperm quality and testosterone levels and negatively affect learning and memory. Plastic can also be part of the cause of hormone driven cancers such as breast and prostate cancer.

How to Reduce Plastic Usage:

In short, follow the wisdom of our beautiful Hawaiian mermaid Kaimana in this book!

Three Steps:

1. DON'T BUY IT UNLESS YOU HAVE TO: Use a more sustainable source of reusable containers or packaging such as metal or glass containers or cloth bags.

2. REUSE IT: IF you have to use it, reuse it as long as possible. (Avoid single-use plastic or get creative.)

3. RECYCLE (if you can, see note below): Once it is no longer useful, make sure it is recycled.

4. A NOTE ABOUT RECYCLING: The general idea is that recycling is environmentally friendly, which is true in the case of plastics labeled #1 and #2. In all other instances, I am sorry to share that all the other plastic containers just end up in the landfill or the ocean. Please don't think recycling will solve the issue at hand! It is shocking to know that less than 10% of all the plastic that has ever been made has actually been recycled. This is a much deeper-rooted issue, where we must look at our addiction to this convenient petroleum product called plastic.

More important tips:

1. Put pressure on oil companies and the government to reduce plastic usage. While it's important as individuals to reduce our plastic addiction, it's important to address the issue on a global scale, which unfortunately stems from oil corporations and big business.

2. Avoid buying single use plastic or buy products that use as little of it as possible. Plastic straws, plates and cutlery make our lives easier, but they have a serious impact on the planet. Instead, use metal and bamboo alternatives, or biodegradable plastics if possible. Choose to buy shampoo, soap, and dish soap as bars in paper or cardboard packaging.

3. If you do buy plastic, make sure it's something important and you have to have it Examine your ideas and belief systems about 'needs' and 'wants'.

4. If you can't recycle it, when you put it in the trash try to make sure it stays in as large a piece as possible, so you don't speed up the breakdown to smaller micro plastics.

5. Buy in bulk – disposable containers are ubiquitous (polystyrene trays, PET bottles, tetra paks, plastic containers, etc) but more and more stores are offering the possibility to buy foods like cereals and rice in bulk.

6. Rethink your food storage – instead of using plastic baggies, plastic wrap and plastic storage containers, try opting for a bento box or tiffin. Instead of using plastic zipper bags or wrapping things in Saran wrap, use jars or glass containers.

7. Take a cloth bag when you go shopping.

8. Shop at a local farmers market – farmers markets are a great way to buy fresh, local produce without plastic, as long as you remember to bring your own bags.
9. Replace plastic Tupperware for glass or steel containers.
10. If you do happen to use any plastics, put your plastic waste in the correct recycling container and in accordance to your local recycling services.
11. Avoid using cosmetics that use microplastics.
12. Buy less clothing and wash them only when necessary- a single wash can cause 700,000 bits of microplastics to be released into the environment.
13. Buy "natural fabrics" like cotton, hemp and linen. Processing these materials is far less water – intensive than synthetic fabrics like polyester and nylon and they will last longer.
14. Use a refillable water bottle.
15. DIY your cleaning products- use a mixture of 1-part vinegar to 3 parts water as an all-purpose spray cleaner (storing it in a reused spray bottle) and produce wash.
16. Try natural beeswax coated cloth wraps instead of plastic cling film
17. Buy necessary plastic items used instead of new.
18. Compost food waste to avoid plastic garbage bags.

Happywhale

As you can tell from reading this book, I am passionate about ocean conservation and the future for our beloved whales. My magnanimous brother, Ted Cheeseman, just happen to be the creator of Happywhale, which uses state-of-the-art image processing algorithms to match whale photos with scientific collections. This newly developed efficiency now makes global whale tracking more possible than ever.

A portion of the proceeds from each book will go to his organization. It seems fitting to collaborate with my brother for such a worthy cause with 'Kaimana the Hawaiian Mermaid'. I know our recently deceased parents would be happy about this too!

Happywhale's mission is to increase global understanding and caring for marine environments through creating high quality conservation science and education.

Happywhale aims to make it easy and rewarding for the public to participate in science. How? By building innovative tools to engage anyone interested in marine mammals and serve the research community with powerful collaborative tools.

Tourism as Science: Ecotourists can be citizen scientists through Happywhale. Have fun learning about your whales while the data in your photos builds our understanding!

Please check out Happywhale at:

www.happywhale.com/home

www.instagram.com/happywhale_official/

www.facebook.com/happywhales

About Hannah Mermaid

Hannah Fraser created the vocation 'Professional Mermaid', making spectacular mermaid tails, performing & speaking for film, tv, events & environmental actions. She creates breathtaking imagery of human & animal encounters with large ocean creatures such as sharks, whales, manta rays and more. She is featured worldwide for her underwater performance art as an advocate for female empowerment and ocean conservation.

To learn more about Hannah, please go to:

www.hannahmermaid.com

About the Illustrator

Nica Quinn is primarily a digital artist but will never confine herself to one medium. She currently resides in Scotland and is constantly inspired by the beautiful country. Nica finds meaning and purpose in drawing a deeper connection to ourselves and nature and animals and through sharing her work and she hopes that it inspires others to do the same.

To learn more about Nica, please go to:

https://www.nicadrawsnature.com/

https://www.instagram.com/nica_draws_nature/

About the Author

Tara Coyote is the author of the best-selling memoir *Grace, Grit & Gratitude: A Cancer Thriver's Journey from Hospice to Full Recovery with the Healing Power of Horses*. She is deeply grateful for the love and wisdom of her horses, which has gotten her through a multitude of challenging experiences.

As her wild mustang Comanche has been such a powerful healing force in her life, Tara is passionate to share this important cause with others to help educate the future generations and their families about wild horses. She is concerned that children of the future will not know what a true mustang is.

She was trained by Linda Kohanov at Eponaquest as an Equine Facilitated Learning teacher and runs a horse retreat center called Wind

Horse Sanctuary which offers private, group sessions and online coaching with horses.

When not writing, teaching, tending to the land and animals, you can find Tara enjoying the tropical beauty of her ancestral homeland of Kaua'i, Hawaii.

To learn more about Tara, please go to:

www.WindHorseSanctuary.com

www.CancerWarrioress.com

www.youtube.com/c/TaraCoyote

www.instagram.com/taracoyote

www.facebook.com/windhorsesanctuary1/

Grace, Grit & Gratitude: A Cancer Thriver's Journey from Hospice to Full Recovery with the Healing Power of Horses - https://amzn.to/3lEJua3

Wind Horse Sanctuary

EQUINE ASSISTED PERSONAL DEVELOPMENT

Mahalo (thank you) for reading my book!

I hope you enjoyed it.

Now that you are finished, I would love your feedback.
Please consider leaving an honest review on Amazon.

Thank you!

Resources

Whale Information:

https://oceanconservancy.org/blog/2022/02/10/sperm-whales/

www.whalefacts.org/why-do-whales-migrate/

www.fisheries.noaa.gov/species/sperm-whale

www.fisheries.noaa.gov/species/humpback-whale

A big mahalo goes out to my beloved brother Ted Cheeseman at happywhale.com/home for his astute knowledge about whales.

Coral Reef Restoration:

www.gbrrestoration.org

www.coralrestoration.org

www.oceanexplorer.noaa.gov/facts/coral-animal.html

Plastic Info:

https://education.nationalgeographic.org/resource/microplastics/

www.earthday.org/fact-sheet-plastics-in-the-ocean/

www.earth.org/ways-to-reduce-your-plastic-waste/

www.oceanservice.noaa.gov/facts/microplastics.html

Many thanks to Martin Webb for his assistance and suggestions for plastic conservation: https://climatemartin.wixsite.com/future-solutions-now

Native Hawaiian Info:

www.letslearnslang.com/origin-of-the-name-kaimana/

Conservation Videos & Resources:

Plastic Pollution and Solutions - A 5-minute video created by Martin Webb and I: https://youtu.be/vXLWP55G2pI?si=UggcpQcp54LBjYxd

Honor the Earth - An award-winning short film equating my stage 4 cancer healing journey with climate change: https://youtu.be/ZbRnsjrK6R8?si=y38ykzV6ARsZbPcY

Resources for the Earth – A page with solutions for how to make a difference for the environment. My environmentalist mother and I created this page the year before she passed. It was the last project she did before she died and it is extra special to me: www.cancerwarrioress.com/resources-earth

Made in the USA
Las Vegas, NV
29 June 2026

49588576R00038